words of grace

words of grace

SELECTED AND EDITED BY JAMES C. GALVIN

Tyndale House Publishers, Inc.
Wheaton, Illinois

Produced with the assistance of The Livingstone Corporation.

Photo by Andrea Gjeldum
Design by Andrea Gjeldum

Spine visual effect compliments of Schwarz Leather Company

Scripture verses are taken from *The Living Bible,* copyright © 1971 owned by assignment by KNT Charitable Trust. All rights reserved.

Typesetting for featured verses designed by Timothy R. Botts. Adapted from the
Life Application Bible for Students, copyright © 1992 by Tyndale House Publishers.

Devotional thoughts adapted from the *Life Application Bible,* copyright © 1986, 1988 by Tyndale House Publishers.

Library of Congress Cataloging-in-Publication Data

Galvin, James C.
  Words of grace / selected and edited by James C. Galvin.
     p.   cm.
  ISBN 0-8423-7929-0 : $6.99
  1. Bible—Meditations.   2. Meditations.   I. Title.
BS483.5.G35 1995   94-40286
242′.5—dc

Printed in the United States of America

00   99   98   97   96   95
6   5   4   3   2   1

IS aNyThIng
TOO
hard
for GOD?

GENESIS 18:14

"Is anything too hard for God?" The obvious answer is, "Of course not!" This question reveals much about God. God is all-powerful. He is almighty. No problem in your life is so big that God is unable to do something about it. When you feel discouraged, try inserting some of your specific needs into the question. "Is this day in my life too hard for the Lord?" "Is this habit I'm trying to break too hard for him?" "Is the communication problem I'm having too hard for him?" Asking the question this way reminds you that God is personally involved in your life and nudges you to ask for his power to help you.

NOW GO AHEAD
AND DO AS
I TELL YOU

for *I will help* **YOU**

то SPEAK WELL

and *I will tell you*

WHAT
WHAT
WHAT
WHAT
W H A T
to say.

EXODUS 4:12

Moses pleaded with God to let him out of his mission. After all, he was not a good speaker and would probably embarrass both himself and God. Moses focused on his weaknesses. But God looked at Moses' problem quite differently. All Moses needed was some help, and who better than God could help him say and do the right things? God made his mouth and would give him the words to say. It is easy for us to focus on our weaknesses, but if God asks us to do something, then we can count on him to help us get the job done. If the job involves some of our weak areas, then we can trust that he will provide words, strength, courage, and ability where needed.

DON'T BE *afraid.*

Just **STAND**

where you are

and **WATCH**

and you will **SEE**

the wonderful way

THE LORD

will rescue you

TODAY.

EXODUS 14:13

The people of Israel were about to escape from Egypt. They found themselves trapped between the Red Sea and the Egyptian army. They quickly became hostile and despairing, but Moses encouraged them to watch the wonderful way God would rescue them. Moses had a positive attitude! When it looked as if they were trapped, Moses called upon God to intervene. We may not be chased by an army, but we may still feel trapped: in a job, in a relationship, or in a financial mess. Instead of giving in to despair, we should adopt Moses' attitude to watch and see what God will do.

HONOR
YOUR FATHER
AND MOTHER
that you may have a
L O N G
Good Life
in the land
THE LORD
YOUR GOD
will give **You.**

EXODUS 20:12

This is the first commandment with a promise attached.
To live in peace for generations in the Promised Land,
the Israelites would need to respect authority and build
strong families. Even those who find it difficult to get
along with their parents are still commanded to honor
them. But what does it mean to "honor" parents? Partly,
it means speaking well of them and politely to them. It
also means acting in a way that shows them courtesy and
respect. It doesn't mean placing our parents ahead of
God (which is why we may have to disobey them if they
are asking us to be disobedient to God). Parents have a
special place in God's sight.

IF **Y**OU*R*
brother
becomes poor,

YOU *are*
RESPONSIBLE
to help him;
invite him
to live
with you
AS A GUEST
IN **Y**OUR HOME.

LEVITICUS 25:35

God said that neglecting the poor was a sin. Permanent poverty was not allowed in Israel. Financially secure families were responsible to help and house those in need. Many times we do nothing, not because we lack compassion, but because we are overwhelmed by the size of the problem and don't know where to begin. God doesn't expect you to eliminate poverty, nor does he expect you to neglect your family while providing for others. He does, however, expect that when you see an individual in need, you will reach out with whatever help you can offer, including hospitality. Don't neglect your responsibility to help a brother or sister in need.

THE LORD
loves

US US US US US US US US US US US US US US US US US US US US US US US US US US US US

HE will bring *us* safely into the land and give it to *us.*

NUMBERS 14:8

Joshua and Caleb pleaded with the people to believe that the Lord would bring them safely into the land. With great miracles, God had led the Israelites out of slavery, through the desolate desert, and up to the very edge of the Promised Land. He had protected them, fed them, and fulfilled every promise. Yet when encouraged to take that last step of faith and enter the land, the people refused. They were afraid.

After witnessing so many miracles, why did they stop trusting God? Why did they refuse to enter the Promised Land when that had been their goal since leaving Egypt? Often we do the same thing: We trust God to handle the smaller issues but doubt his ability to take care of the big problems, the tough decisions, the frightening situations. Don't stop trusting God just as you are ready to reach your goal. He brought you this far and won't let you down now.

CHOOSE
TO *LOVE*
THE LORD
YOUR GOD
and to
OBEY HIM
and to
CLING
TO HIM,
for HE *IS*
your life.

DEUTERONOMY 30:20

Moses urged the Israelites to choose to love the Lord, obey him, and cling to him. This is the response of faith. In contrast, the world hates God, chooses to disobey his commands, and wants total independence. One way ends in life and the other in death. God makes the choice clear because he wants us all to choose life. Daily, in each new situation, we must affirm and reinforce this commitment. Each day we can choose to love God more deeply, obey him more fully, and cling to him more tightly.

I WILL <u>NOT</u>
a b a n d o n   YOU
or fail
to help YOU.

JOSHUA 1:5

Joshua's new job consisted of leading more than two million people into a strange new land and conquering it. What a challenge—even for a man of Joshua's caliber! Every new job is a challenge. Without God it can be frightening. With God it can be a great adventure. Just as God was with Joshua, he is with us as we face our new challenges. We may not conquer nations, but every day we face tough situations, difficult people, and temptations. However, God promises that he will never abandon us or fail to help us. By asking God to direct us, we can conquer many of life's challenges.

BE **BOLD** AND **STRONG!**

Remember,

THE LORD YOUR GOD
is with YOU

w h e r e v e r   y o u   g o.

JOSHUA 1:9

When God commissioned Joshua, he told him three times to be bold and strong. Apparently Joshua took God's message to heart. He confidently led the people across the Jordan River and bravely led the warriors in conquest of the cities in the land. Joshua trusted God and found the strength and courage he needed to fulfill his duties. The next time you are afraid to do what you know is right, remember that strength and courage are readily available from God. He is fully able to give you all the courage you need to face each day and each new challenge.

"Don't make me
l e a v e you,
FOR
I want to go wherever you go, and to
live
wherever
you live;

YOUR PEOPLE
shall be MY PEOPLE,
A N D
YOUR GOD
shall be MY GOD."

RUTH 1:16

Ruth was a Moabitess, but that didn't stop her from worshiping the true God, nor did it stop God from accepting her worship and blessing her greatly. God accepts all who worship him; he works through people regardless of their race, sex, or nationality. The book of Ruth is a perfect illustration of God's love for all nations. Although Ruth belonged to a race often despised by Israel, she was blessed because of her faithfulness. She became a great-grandmother of King David and a direct ancestor of Jesus. No one should feel disqualified to serve God because of race, sex, or national background. God can use anyone to build his kingdom.

Don't judge BY

a man's face OR

I don't make HEIGHT...

DECISIONS
DECISIONS

the way you do!

MEN *judge* BY

OUTWARD APPEARANCE.

BUT

I LOOK

AT A MAN'S

thoughts

AND
INTENTIONS.

1 SAMUEL 16:7

When Samuel went to Bethlehem to anoint the next king of Israel, God warned him against judging by appearance alone. Appearance doesn't reveal what people are really like or their true value. Fortunately, God judges by faith and character, not mere outward appearances. And because only God can see on the inside, only he can accurately judge people. Most likely, you spend several hours each week maintaining your outward appearance; why not spend even more time developing your inner character? While everyone can see your face, only you and God know what your heart really looks like. What steps are you taking to improve your thoughts and intentions?

AND *AFTER* THE

EARTHQUAKE

THERE WAS A *fire*,

BUT THE LORD
*WAS **NOT*** IN THE
fire.

AND *AFTER* THE *fire*,

THERE WAS
THE SOUND OF
A GENTLE
WHISPER.

1 KING 19:12

When Elijah was hiding in a cave at Mount Horeb, he experienced a mighty windstorm, an earthquake, and a fire, but God was not in these awesome displays of his power. Then Elijah heard the sound of a gentle whisper and went outside. He knew that the gentle whisper was God's voice. He realized that God doesn't reveal himself only in powerful, miraculous ways. If you look for God only in some big event or miraculous display of power, you may miss him because he is often found gently whispering in the quietness of a humbled heart. Are you listening for God? Step back from the noise and activity of your busy life and listen humbly and quietly for his guidance.

IF MY PEOPLE
will
humble
themselves
AND pray,
AND
search for me,
AND
TURN FROM their
wicked ways,
I WILL
HEAR THEM
FROM HEAVEN AND
forgive
their sins
AND
heal their land.

2 CHRONICLES 7:14

Solomon asked God to make provisions for the people when they sinned. Solomon asked that God would hear their prayers and help them. God answered with four conditions for forgiveness: ⌐1⌐ humble yourself, ⌐2⌐ pray to God, asking for forgiveness, ⌐3⌐ seek God continually, and ⌐4⌐ turn from sinful behavior. True repentance is more than talk—it is changed behavior. Whether we sin individually, as a group, or as a nation, following these steps will lead to forgiveness. God will answer our earnest prayers.

WHO
WHO
WHO
CAN SAY BUT THAT
GOD
has brought
you
into the
PALACE
for just
such
a time
as
this?

ESTHER 4:14

After the decree to kill the Jews was given, Mordecai and Esther could have despaired, decided to save only themselves, or just waited for God's intervention. Instead, they saw that God had placed them in their positions for a purpose, so they seized the moment and acted. When it is within our reach to help others, we must do so. Don't withdraw, behave selfishly, wallow in despair, or wait for God to fix everything. Instead, ask God for his direction, and *act!* God may have placed you where you are "for just such a time as this."

heavens
heavens
The heavens
heavens
heavens
ARE TELLING
THE GLORY OF GOD
THE GLORY OF GOD
THE GLORY OF GOD
THE GLORY OF

They are a
marvelous
of his   display
CRAFTSMANSHIP.

PSALM 19:1

We are surrounded by fantastic displays of God's crafts-manship—the heavens give dramatic evidence of his existence, his power, his love, and his care. To say that the universe happened by chance is absurd. Its design, intricacy, and orderliness point to a personally involved Creator. As you look at God's handiwork in nature and the heavens, thank him for such magnificent beauty and the truth it reveals about the Creator.

Because

THE LORD

is

MY SHEPHERD

I have

EVeRyTHing

I need!

The New Testament calls Jesus the Good Shepherd (John 10:11); the great Shepherd (Hebrews 13:20); and the Head Shepherd (1 Peter 5:4). As the Lord is the Good Shepherd, so we are his sheep—not frightened, passive animals, but obedient followers, wise enough to follow one who will lead us in the right places and in right ways. Sheep are completely dependent on the shepherd for provision, guidance, and protection. We are better disciples when we are dependent upon Jesus. When you recognize the Good Shepherd, follow him!

GO
THROUGH
H I S
O P E N
G A T E S
with **GREAT**
thanksgiving

ENTER HIS COURTS
with
P R A I S E
P R A I S E
P R A I S E

Give thanks to HIM
and
BLESS BLESS BLESS BLESS
HIS NAME

PSALM 100:4

What is your attitude toward worship? Do you willingly and joyfully come into God's presence, or are you just going through the motions, reluctantly attending the church services? This psalm tells us to remember God's goodness and dependability and then to worship with thanksgiving and praise! It's easy to enter the church sanctuary with complaints and thoughts of everything you want to do when you get back home. But this psalm tells us to enter his courts with praise and give him thanks as we go in.

If **YOU** *want* FAVOR
with
BOTH GOD and man,
and a REPUTATION
for
GOOD JUDGMENT
and
common sense,
T H E N
trust THE LORD
C O M P L E T E L Y

DON'T EVER TRUST
YOURSELF.

In
everything
YOU *do*
PUT GOD FIRST
and
HE *will direct* **YOU**
and
CROWN YOUR EFFORTS
with *SUCCESS*

PROVERBS 3:4-6

To succeed, said Solomon, we must put God first in our life, trusting in him completely. This means turning every area of life over to him. About a thousand years later, Jesus emphasized this same truth (Matthew 6:33). Look at your values and priorities. What is important to you? In what areas have you not acknowledged God? What is his advice? Make him a vital part of everything you do; then he will direct you and crown your efforts with success because you will be working to accomplish his purposes.

There are
"friends"
who pretend to be
friends,
BUT
there is a *Friend*
who sticks
closer
than a brother

PROVERBS 18:24

Loneliness is everywhere—many people feel cut off and alienated from others. Being in a crowd just makes people more aware of their isolation. We all need friends who will stick close, listen, care, and offer help when it is needed—in good times and bad. It is better to have one such friend than dozens of superficial acquaintances. But how can a person find a friend like this? Instead of wishing you could *find* a true friend, seek to *become* one. There are people around you who need your friendship. Ask God to reveal them to you, and then take on the challenge of being a true friend.

HE *was* wounded
AND bruised
FOR **O**UR sins.
HE *was* beaten
THAT
WE *MIGHT* HAVE
P E A C E ;
HE *was* lashed
AND
WE *were* *healed!*

ISAIAH 53:5

This verse predicts what was going to happen to Jesus in his suffering and death for our sins. How could someone in the Old Testament understand the idea of Christ dying for our sins and actually bearing the punishment that we deserved? The sacrifices suggested this idea—but it is one thing to kill a lamb, and something quite different to think of God's chosen servant as that Lamb. Through this prophecy, God was pulling aside the curtain of time to let the people of Isaiah's day look ahead to the suffering of the future Messiah and the resulting forgiveness that would be made available to the whole world. Through the Bible, we have the double benefit of knowing both the prophecy and the fulfillment in Christ.

FOR
I KNOW
T H E P L A N S
I HAVE
for YOU,
says
THE LORD.
They are
P L A N S
for GOOD
AND **NOT** *for* **evil**,
to give YOU
A FUTURE
AND A HOPE.

JEREMIAH 29:11

We're all encouraged by a leader who stirs us to move ahead—someone who believes we can do the task he has given and who will be with us all the way. God is that kind of leader. He knows the future, and his plans for us are good. As long as God, who knows the future, provides our agenda and goes with us as we fulfill his mission, we can have boundless hope. This does not mean that we will be spared pain, suffering, or hardship, but it does mean that God will see us through to a glorious conclusion.

GREAT
is
HIS
FAITHFULNESS
HIS *loving-kindness*
BEGINS AFRESH

EACH DAY
EACH DAY
EACH DAY
EACH DAY
EACH DAY

LAMENTATIONS 3:23

Jeremiah knew from personal experience about God's faithfulness. God had promised that punishment would follow disobedience, and it did. But God had also promised future restoration and blessing, and Jeremiah knew that God would keep that promise too. Each morning can remind us of God's faithfulness when we consider the blessings he has given us for that day. Trusting in God's faithfulness day by day makes us confident in his great promises for the future.

I will give you
a new heart
I will give you
new and right desires
and put a new spirit
within you
I will give you
new hearts of
LOVE

EZEKIEL 36:26

God promised to restore Israel not only physically but also spiritually. To accomplish this, God would give them a new heart for following him and put his Spirit within them to transform them and empower them to do his will. This New Covenant promise would ultimately be fulfilled in Christ. No matter how impure your life is right now, God offers you a fresh start. You can have your sins washed away, receive a new heart for God, and have his Spirit within you—if you simply believe and accept God's promise. Why try to patch up your old life when you can have a brand-new one?

THOSE
WHO ARE WISE
SHALL SHINE
AS BRIGHTLY AS
THE SUN'S BRILLIANCE
and
THOSE
who turn
many to
RIGHTEOUSNESS
Will glitter
like stars
f o r e v e r

DANIEL 12:3

Many people try to be stars in the world of entertainment, only to find their stardom temporary. God tells us how we can be eternal "stars"—by being wise and leading others to God's righteousness. Part of God's plan for the salvation of the world is that he uses us to tell the gospel to the world. He produces the conversion; we simply serve as his messengers of this Good News. If we share our Lord with others, we can be true stars—radiantly beautiful in God's sight!

Oh
that
we might
know THE
LORD
LET US PRESS ON
TO KNOW HIM
and
HE will
respond
to Us
as
surely as

THE COMING OF DAWN
THE COMING OF DAWN
or the rain
of early spring

HOSEA 6:3

God had shown his faithfulness to Israel many times. They knew that if they sought to know him and his ways, he would reveal himself to them, and they were right. The problem was that they were so deep in sin, they did not really want to know him. They wanted God's blessings, but not his discipline or guidance. The people of Israel were more interested in the material benefits God provided than in the eternal benefits he wanted to give them. Consider your own attitude. What do you hope to get from God? Do you repent with little intention of changing your life? Do you really want to know God? God wants you to press on to know him.

I will pour out
my Spirit
upon

ALL OF YOU
ALL OF YOU
ALL OF YOU

YOUR SONS
and daughters
WILL PROPHESY
YOUR
OLD MEN
will dream
dreams
and
YOUR YOUNG MEN
SEE VISIONS
SEE VISIONS
SEE VISIONS
SEE VISIONS

JOEL 2:28

The apostle Peter quoted this verse in Acts 2:16-21—the outpouring of the Spirit predicted by Joel occurred on Pentecost. While in the past God's Spirit was primarily active in the lives of kings, prophets, or judges, Joel envisioned a time when the Spirit would be available to every believer. God's Spirit is available now to anyone who calls on him. Take some time to consider how different your life would be without the Holy Spirit empowering you to do his will. Thank God today for the work of his Spirit in your life.

GOD HAS TOLD YOU
WHAT HE *wants,*
and this is all it is:
to be FAIR
and JUST
and *merciful,*
and to
w a l k h u m b l y
with YOUR GOD.

from MICAH 6:8

People have tried all kinds of ways to please God, but God has made his wishes clear: He wants his people to be fair, just, and merciful, and to walk humbly with him. He does not want us to sacrifice *things* to him—he wants us to become *living* sacrifices (Romans 12:1). In your efforts to please God, examine these areas on a regular basis. Are you fair in your dealings with people? Are you concerned when injustice is done? Do you show mercy to those who wrong you? Are you learning humility?

THE
LORD GOD
IS MY
STRENGTH;

*HE WILL
GIVE ME
THE SPEED*

OF A DEER

and bring me safely over

THE
MOUNTAINS.

HABAKKUK 3:19

God has promised that he will give his followers sure-footed confidence through difficult times. They will run like deer across rough and dangerous terrain. At the proper time, God will bring about his justice and completely rid the world of evil. In the meantime, God's people need to live in the strength of his Spirit, confident in his ultimate victory. Don't be discouraged by the mountains you face in life, but let them be opportunities for God to give you more of his strength and speed.

NOT by **MIGHT**
NOR by *POWER*
B U T
by
My Spirit
SAYS THE LORD
ALMIGHTY

ZECHARIAH 4:6

Many people believe that to survive in this world a person must be tough, strong, unbending, and harsh. But God says, "You will succeed because of my Spirit, though you are few and weak." The key words are "because of my Spirit." It is *only* through God's Spirit that anything of lasting value is accomplished. The returned exiles were indeed weak—harassed by their enemies, tired, discouraged, and poor. But they had God on their side! As you live for God, determine not to trust in your own strength or abilities. Instead, depend on God and work in the power of his Spirit!

And
she will
have a Son,

and you shall
name him `JESUS`

(meaning "Savior"),

for **he will save**
his people

from their
sins sins sins
sins sins sins
sins sins sins

MATTHEW 1:21

Jesus means "Savior." Jesus came to earth to save us because we couldn't save ourselves from sin and its consequences. No matter how good we are, we can't eliminate our sinful nature. Only Jesus can do that. Jesus didn't come to help people save themselves; he came to be their Savior from the power and penalty of sin. Thank Christ for his death on the cross that took away the penalty for your sin. Thank him for the power he gives you to live a new life. Thank him that you will one day be free from all sin when you are with him in heaven.

ALL
WHO LISTEN
TO MY
INSTRUCTIONS
AND F O L L O W THEM
ARE WISE,
LIKE
A MAN
WHO BUILDS
HIS HOUSE
ON SOLID
ROCK

MATTHEW 7:24

Like a house of cards, the fool's life crumbles. Most people do not deliberately seek to build on a false or inferior foundation; instead, they just don't think about their life's purpose. Many people are headed for destruction not out of stubbornness but out of carelessness. It's easier to dig and build on sand than it is on rock, but when storms come, the sand is a pretty shaky base. Listen to God's instructions for life and follow them. This is the only way to build your life on solid rock.

"*Go home
to your
friends,*"
JESUS told him,
"and tell them
WHAT
WONDERFUL
THINGS
GOD *has done*
for YOU;
and HOW
merciful
m e r c i f u l
m e r c i f u l
HE*has been.*"

MARK 5:19

This demon-possessed man became a living example of Jesus' power. He wanted to go with Jesus, but Jesus told him to go home and share his story with his friends. If you have experienced Jesus' power, you too are a living example of it. Are you, like this man, enthusiastic about sharing the Good News with those around you? Just as we would tell others about a doctor who provided the cure for a physical disease, we should tell them about Christ, who provided the "cure" for our sin.

EVERyOne
WHO
asks,
RECEIVES;
All WHO seek,
FIND;
AND THE
DOOR is
OPENED
TO EVERyOne
WHO knocks.

LUKE 11:10

Jesus told a parable about a man who needed bread and knocked on the door of a neighbor's house until he received it. He told us to keep asking, looking, and knocking when we pray. Practicing persistence does more to change *our* heart and mind than his, and it helps us understand and express the intensity of our need. Persistence in prayer helps us recognize God's work. How persistent in prayer have you been lately?

WHY ARE
YOU looking in a
TOMB
FOR
SOMEONE
WHO IS alive?
HE isn't HERE!

HE has
come back
to life again!

LUKE 24:5-6

After Jesus had died, several of the women went to the tomb to take care of his body. Two angels who appeared as men "clothed in shining robes" asked the women why they were looking in a tomb for someone who was alive. Often we run into people who are looking for God among the dead. They study the Bible as a mere historical document and go to church as if going to a memorial service. But Jesus is not among the dead—he lives! He reigns in the hearts of Christians, and he is the head of his church. Do you look for Jesus among the living? Do you expect him to be active in the world and in the church? Look for signs of his power—they are all around you.

JESUS
told him,
"I AM
THE **WAY**–
YES, AND
THE **TRUTH**
AND THE **LIFE.**
NO ONE CAN GET TO
THE FATHER
EXCEPT BY MEANS OF

JOHN 14:6

ME."

Jesus says he is the Way, the Truth, and the Life. As the *Way,* Jesus is our path to the Father. As the *Truth,* he is the reality of all God's promises. As the *Life,* he joins his divine life to ours, both now and eternally. Some object that Jesus can't be the *only* way to the Father because that is too narrow. In reality, the way is wide enough for the whole world, if the world chooses to accept it. Instead of worrying about how limited it sounds to have only one way, we should be happy that God has provided a sure way for us to get to him.

But when
THE HOLY SPIRIT
has come upon you,

You will receive

POWER
to TESTIFY

about ME
with
GREAT
EFFECT
E F F E C T T
F F E C

ACTS 1:8

Jesus had instructed his disciples to witness to people of all nations about him (Matthew 28:19-20). But they were told to wait first for the Holy Spirit (Luke 24:49). God has important work for you to do for him, but you must do it by the power of the Holy Spirit. We often want to get on with the job, even if it means running ahead of God. But waiting is sometimes part of God's plan. Are you waiting and listening for God's complete instructions? We need God's timing and power to be truly effective in sharing our faith—and anything else he calls us to do.

NO TEMPTATION
IS IRRESISTIBLE.

You can trust GOD
to keep
the
TEMPTATION
FROM BECOMING
SO STRONG

that you can't
stand up
against it,

for
HE *has*
promised this
and *will do*
what HE says.

HE *will show*
you
how to
e s c a p e

1 CORINTHIANS 10:13

In a culture filled with moral depravity and sin-inducing pressures, Paul gave strong encouragement to the Corinthians about temptation. He said: [1] everyone has wrong desires and temptations, so don't feel you've been singled out; [2] others have resisted temptation, and so can you; and [3] any temptation can be resisted because God will help you resist it. God helps you resist temptation by helping you [1] recognize those people and situations that give you trouble, [2] run from anything you know is wrong, [3] choose to do only what is right, [4] pray for his help, and [5] seek friends who love him and can offer help when you are tempted.

WHEN
SOMEONE
becomes
A CHRISTIAN
HE becomes
A BRAND NEW
PERSON
inside.
HE is not the same any more.
A
new life
has begun!

2 CORINTHIANS 5:17

Christians are brand-new people on the *inside*. The Holy Spirit gives them new life, and they are not the same anymore. We are not reformed, rehabilitated, or re-educated—we are new creations, living in vital union with Christ (Colossians 2:6-7). At conversion we are not merely turning over a new leaf; we are beginning a new life under a new Master. Don't let yourself be enslaved to old habits and sins. Determine to live like the new person you are.

G<small>OD</small> *said,* I AM WITH YOU

That is all you need.

M<small>Y</small>
POWER
shows up BEST in
weak people.

NOW
I AM GLAD to *BOAST*
about HOW *weak* I AM;

I AM GLAD to be

A LIVING DEMONSTRATION OF
CHRIST'S POWER
instead of
SHOWING OFF
MY OWN POWER
AND ABILITIES

2 CORINTHIANS 12:9

Paul asked God for relief from an affliction (we aren't sure what it was), and God denied his request. Although God did not remove Paul's physical affliction, he promised to show his power through Paul. The fact that God's power is displayed in weaknesses should give us courage. We must rely on God for our effectiveness rather than simply on our own energy, effort, or talent. Our weakness not only helps develop Christian character but also deepens our worship, because in admitting our weakness, we affirm God's strength.

BUT when the
HOLY SPIRIT
CONTROLS
OUR LIVES
HE *will produce*
this kind of fruit in **U**s:

Love O
J JOY Y
J O Y

PEACE

P A T I E N C E

kindness

Goodness

FAITHFULNESS

gentleness

SELF-CONTROL.

GALATIANS 5:22,23

The Spirit produces in us these character traits that are found in the nature of Christ. They are the by-products of Christ's control—if we want the fruit of the Spirit to grow in us, we must join our life to his (see John 15:4-5). We must know him, love him, remember him, and imitate him. As a result, we will fulfill the intended purpose of the law—to love God and our neighbors. Which of these qualities do you most want the Spirit to produce in you at this time?

*May you be able to feel
and understand,*
as all God's children should,

HOW L O N   G

HOW WIDE

HOW DEEP

and HOW HIGH

HIS LOVE *really is;
and to experience this LOVE
for yourselves....*

AND SO AT L A S   T
you will be filled up with
GOD HIMSELF.

EPHESIANS 3:18-19

God's love is total, says Paul. It reaches every corner of our experience. God's love is *long*—it continues the length of our lives. It is *wide*—it covers the breadth of our own experience, and it reaches out to the whole world. His love is *deep*—it reaches to the depths of discouragement, despair, and even death. It is *high*—it rises to the heights of our celebration and elation. When you feel shut out or isolated, remember that you can never be lost to God's love.

I CAN DO
EVeRYTHING
GOD asks ME to
with the help of CHRIST
who gives
gives
gives
gives ME
the
STRENGTH
and
POWER

PHILIPPIANS 4:13

Can we really do everything? The power we receive from Christ is sufficient to do his will and to face the challenges that arise from our commitment to doing it. He does not grant us superhuman ability to accomplish anything we can imagine without regard to his interests. As you contend for the faith, you will face troubles, pressures, and trials. As they come, ask Christ to strengthen you.

WORK *hard* and *cheerfully* at A L L *you do,* just as though *you were* **working** for THE LORD.

Since the Creation, God has given us work to do. If we could regard our work as an act of worship or service to God, such an attitude would take some of the drudgery and boredom out of it. Don't complain about your job. Don't be downcast when you have a lot to do. Work hard and be cheerful, as though the Lord were your direct supervisor.

ALWAYS KEEP ON PRAYING
ALWAYS KEEP ON PRAYING
ALWAYS KEEP ON PRAYING
ALWAYS KEEP ON PRAYING
ALWAYS KEEP ON PRAYING
ALWAYS KEEP ON

We cannot spend all our time on our knees, but it is possible to have a prayerful attitude at all times. This attitude is built upon acknowledging our dependence on God, recognizing his presence within us, and determining to obey him fully. Then we will find it natural to pray frequent, spontaneous, short prayers. A prayerful attitude is not a substitute for regular times of prayer but an outgrowth of those times.

DON'T let a n y o n e
think little of **YOU**

because YOU *are* young.

BE their IDEAL;
let them *follow the way*
you teach and live;

BE a PATTERN

for them in
YOUR LOVE
YOUR FAITH
and YOUR CLEAN THOUGHTS

1 TIMOTHY 4:12

Timothy was a young pastor. It would have been easy for older Christians to look down on him because of his youth. He had to earn the respect of his elders by setting an example in his speech, life, love, faith, and purity. Regardless of your age, God can use you. Whether you are young or old, don't think of your age as a handicap. Live so others can see Christ in you.

THE WHOLE BIBLE
WAS GIVEN TO US
BY INSPIRATION FROM GOD

and is useful to teach us
what is TRUE
and to make us realize
what is wrong
in our lives;
IT
straightens us out
and helps us do
what is RIGHT.

2 TIMOTHY 3:16-17

In our zeal for the *truth* of Scripture, we must never forget its *purpose*—to help us do what is right. We should not study God's Word simply to increase our knowledge or to prepare us to win arguments. We should study the Bible so that we will know how to do Christ's work in the world.

A Person
who is
PURE of heart
SEES
GOODNESS
and P U R I T Y
everything in
EVERYTHING
EVERYTHING everything
everything;
BUT
A Person
whose own heart is
evil
and
untrusting
finds
EVERY
IN evil THING
IN evil
e v RY
IN e v i l
IN THe H I N G
EVERY THING

TITUS 1:15

Some people see good all around them, while others see nothing but evil. What is the difference? Our soul becomes a filter through which we perceive goodness or evil. The pure learn to see goodness and purity even in this evil world. But corrupt and unbelieving people find evil in everything because their evil mind and heart color even the good they see and hear. Whatever you choose to fill your mind with will affect the way you think and act. Turn your thoughts to God and his Word, and you will discover more and more goodness, even in this evil world. A mind filled with good has little room for what is evil.

For since
HE <u>HIMSELF</u>

has now
been through
suffering
and temptation,
HE
knows
what
it is like
when
WE suffer
and are tempted,
and
HE *is*
wonderfully able
to help us.

HEBREWS 2:18

Knowing that Christ suffered pain and faced temptation helps us face our trials. Jesus understands our struggles because he faced them as a human being. When you face trials, go to Jesus for strength and patience. He understands your needs and is able to help.

SO LET US COME
BOLDLY
TO THE
VERY
THRONE
OF GOD
and stay there

to receive

his mercy

and
to find

grace
grace *e*
e
grace *c*
to
g help *c*
r us in *a* *e*
our
t i m e s
of need
.

HEBREWS 4:16

Prayer is our approach to God, and we are to come boldly. Some Christians approach God meekly with heads hung low, afraid to ask him to meet their needs. Others pray flippantly, giving little thought to what they say. Both of these demonstrate a lack of faith on our part. Come with reverence because he is your King. But also come with bold assurance because he is your Friend and Counselor.

DON'T EVER FORGET that it is BEST to LISTEN MUCH SPEAK LITTLE and **not** become ANGRY.

JAMES 1:19

When we talk too much and listen too little, we communicate to others that we think our ideas are much more important than theirs. James wisely advises us to reverse this process. Put a mental stopwatch on your conversations, and keep track of how much you talk and how much you listen. When people talk with you, do they feel that their viewpoints and ideas have value?

I HAVE BEEN
STANDING
AT THE DOOR
AND I AM
C O N S T A N T L Y
K N O C K I N G .

If anyone hears me CALLING HIM and opens the door, I will come in and fellowship with him and he with ME.

REVELATION 3:20

Jesus wants to have fellowship with us, and he wants us to open up to him. He is patient and persistent in trying to get through to us—not breaking and entering, but knocking. He allows us to decide whether or not to open our life to him. Do you intentionally keep his life-changing presence and power on the other side of the door?

HE *will w i p e a w a y*
all te_{ars}
fr_{om} t_he_{ir} e_ye_{s,}
and
there
shall be
NO MORE DEATH,

n_or s_orr_ow,
nor c_ry_in_{g,}
nor *p_ai_{n.}*

ALL
OF THAT
HAS GONE

REVELATION 21:4

F O R E   V   E   R

Have you ever wondered what heaven will be like? The "Holy City, the new Jerusalem" is described as the place where God will "wipe away all tears from their eyes." Forevermore, there will be no death, pain, sorrow, or crying. What a wonderful truth! No matter what you are going through, it's not the last word—God has written the final chapter, and it is about true fulfillment and eternal joy for those who love him. We do not know as much as we would like, but it is enough to know that eternity with God will be more wonderful than we could ever imagine.

Additional Books from
The Livingstone Corporation

101 QUESTIONS CHILDREN ASK ABOUT GOD 0-8423-5102-7
101 QUESTIONS CHILDREN ASK ABOUT THE BIBLE 0-8423-4570-1
Concise, thoughtful, easy-to-explain answers to some of the most
important questions kids will ever ask.

40 FUN BIBLE PUZZLES FOR KIDS Volumes 1-4 *(New! Spring 1995)*
Discover fun and exciting ways to teach the Bible.
   #1 0-8423-1742-2
   #2 0-8423-1743-0
   #3 0-8423-1744-9
   #4 0-8423-1745-7

AFTER-DINNER DEVOTIONS *(New! Spring 1995)* 0-8423-1671-X
A great devotional tool for real-life dilemmas kids face every day